Contact the author:
heidirsugden@gmail.com | instagram: heidi.sugden

Contact the publisher:
Unprecedented Press LLC - 495 Sleepy Hollow Ln, Holland, MI 49423
www.unprecedentedpress.com | info@unprecedentedpress.com
twitter: @UnprecdntdPress | instagram: unprecedentedpress

ISBN-13: 978-1-7321964-1-4
ISBN-10: 1-7321964-1-9

Printed in the United States of America
Ingram Printing & Distribution, 2018

Edited by Thi Dalley
Cover Art by Heidi Sugden

First Edition

Unprecedented
Press

INDISPENSABLE

*small stories
are worth telling*

HEIDI SUGDEN

TABLE OF CONTENTS

To my husband, Tyler, who told me at the beginning of our marriage that I was going to write a book one day. Thank you for seeing my potential and believing in me before I even believed in myself.

There is no prerequisite that says you must have a dramatic testimony for God to use you in powerful ways.

PREFACE

Hummingbirds have always fascinated me. They are amongst the smallest warm-blooded animals on earth, but they're also some of the most remarkable. From a quick glance, they appear delicate and trivial, but the value they hold goes far beyond what meets the eye.

As most probably know, hummingbirds are extremely agile and fast. A hummingbird's wings beat around 80 times per second. You might want to read that sentence again... I didn't say 80 times per minute, but per *second!* This allows them to fly backwards, upside down, and hover in one place. (Oh, and they are the only type of birds who can do this successfully, by the way.) But not only are they incredibly powerful little creatures, they are also extremely valuable when it comes to the task of pollinating flowers.

Over 8,000 species of flowers in the rainforest of South America rely on hummingbirds to pollinate them. Being warm-blooded puts hummingbirds at an advantage. They can fly in cold and rainy conditions, when cold-blooded bees, butterflies and other insect pollinators' wings are too weak to withstand the rain. This makes hummingbirds not only remarkable, but also incredibly necessary.

I'm telling you all this to establish my point that power doesn't always come from volume, quantity or magnitude. There is no prerequisite that says you must have a dramatic testimony for God to use you in powerful ways. Just as the small hummingbird plays a necessary role in its own little sphere of the world, so do you. Your testimony and your voice are necessary. God created you to play an indispensable role in the body of Christ.

1 Corinthians 12:22-24 (NIV) says,

> *"On the contrary, the parts of the body that seem to be weaker are indispensable, and the parts that we think are less honorable, we treat with special honor. And the parts that are unpresentable are treated with special modesty, while our presentable parts need no special treatment."*

God created each of us with a unique purpose in mind, and oh, how I believe that he longs for us to see that "small" is necessary and powerful, too!

My little heart took
the command "say
something" as a command
to prove my significance
—as if being myself
wasn't enough.

1

THE "QUIET" ONE

I remember the day clearly. I was on a field trip with my preschool class and we were at a local park playing on a playground. I don't remember much of what happened before this, but I can clearly recall being surrounded by my classmates. They were all staring at me. After a few moments, one little boy broke the silence and commanded, *"Heidi, say something."* I whimpered a small *"Hi"* and everyone gasped. *"She speaks!"* they all exclaimed. I hung my head in embarrassment as they kept marveling over the realization that I wasn't, in fact, mute.

My mom had told me the night before that I was going to start preschool the next day. My little mind was going a million miles per minute trying to comprehend what preschool even was, let alone what to expect. I don't think that I got any sleep that night. I cried and cried when my mom left me at the school, and once I stopped crying, I kept to myself. As the day went on, I noticed that I really had to use the restroom. We were in the middle of a lesson, and I didn't want to interrupt my teacher in front of everyone to ask permission… so I held it as long as I could until I couldn't hold it anymore. And yes, I peed my pants on the first day of preschool, not because I had issues with my bladder, but because I was too afraid to ask a simple question.

In preschool, I barely said a word to anyone. I was an extremely quiet child, keeping mostly to myself and my own thoughts… so much so that my classmates were surprised when I uttered a single word, and I peed my pants because I was too afraid to speak up. I used to tell these stories as jokes. I used to make light of them and hope that others would see how different I am now than I was back then. I hoped that by seeing how far I had come, it would help me escape the labels "quiet" or "shy." But the truth is, deep down I never found these stories funny. These memories were and are painful for me to remember, because there is still a part of me that identifies with that little girl. From an early age, a wound in me began to form. My little heart took the command "say something" as a command to prove my significance – as if being myself wasn't enough.

The longer I was in school, the more comfortable I got with making friends and talking with my classmates. However, the wound that was deeply imprinted upon me so early on didn't just disappear. The older I got, the more it grew and manifested. What stemmed from being quiet was also an aversion to risk and an uncertainty about myself. I didn't like moving outside my comfort zone and for most of my childhood and teen years, I stayed there – in my safe bubble. At a young age, I remember feeling ashamed when I would hear my Bible school teachers talk about being bold for Jesus. I loved Jesus. So much so that at 4 years old, I asked him into my heart. I knew I wanted that for myself, but being bold and sharing it with others? I didn't think I had it in me. I was too fearful to leave my comfort zone. This left me silent in many situations when I should have spoken up. Instead of seeing this as something that I could change, I internalized it as shame. I was ashamed of who I was, because who I was wasn't enough.

High school came and although I gained friends and a little more confidence, I still found myself categorized as quiet and shy. No matter how hard I tried, I couldn't escape these labels. I used to joke with people that even if I walked around and introduced myself to every stranger in the room and yelled at the top of my lungs, people would still call me "quiet" and "shy." That was a joke, but it also revealed how desperate I was to prove my significance and to be accepted for who I was.

"Why don't you talk very much?" "Why are you so quiet?" "You never say anything." I heard these exact words from so many people in school. How is a girl supposed to interpret that? They may as well have been asking, *"What's wrong with you?"* because that's how I internalized it. And what kind of answer do you give that question anyway? It was just me being me. It was like trying to answer the question, *"Why is the sky blue?"* I should have just said, *"Because God made me this way."* But my insecure heart and mind hadn't internalized that truth quite yet.

How do you describe a million "little" God moments in five minutes? You can't. Yet this is what makes my story, my story.

2

A "Mediocre" Testimony

College wasn't a huge transition as I decided to stay home and attend the local university. The transition for me took place more so in my heart than in my surroundings. During this time, I began to drift away from my friends who were in the midst of pursuing the college experience; and I started to gain an earnest desire to grow closer to God and to know him more fully.

I tried out a few college ministries before ending up back at my home church and their college ministry. After going to a few of the small group nights and with some encouragement from some of the other college kids there, I decided to take the plunge and go on their upcoming spring break trip. I gained so many new friendships and was blown away by the fellowship that existed within this group. I had never experienced such a strong sense of Christian community. After getting a taste of it, I was all in. I started volunteering to help out with events and went to almost every planned or impromptu hang out. I spent most of my free time with these people. We became family. We all cared for, loved, and encouraged one another in an authentic way.

This community was really where my faith began to significantly grow and develop. It was where I chose to pursue God for myself – without my parent's prompting, and where I began to foster my personal relationship with Jesus. God became a part of my everyday thoughts. I would talk to him on my way to and from class, and I began to hear him speak to me in all sorts of ways. His voice would come in the form of a mentor's words, in the soft rustle of the leaves, or in the acts of love that I saw portrayed within our community. It was an amazing discovery to realize I had the ability to hear God's voice. From life-changing decisions to small, everyday dilemmas, I found he had something to say about it all.

To this day, I look back on my faith story and see these little moments of God speaking as what defines my testimony. For me, there was no "breaking point," "turning point" or "rock bottom" like so many others describe. I never turned my back on God. Growing up, I knew the name "Jesus" before I even understood who he was. Did I stray? Definitely. I wasn't perfect, and I did sacrifice some of my values as a teenager, but I never ventured off the deep end. My story has, for the most part, been fairly "mediocre." My lows haven't been that low and my highs haven't been that high. I still find myself struggling to tell my testimony, because it is impossible to tell with a beginning, middle and end. How do you describe a million "little" God moments in five minutes? You can't. Yet this is what makes my story, *my story*.

Because of my "mediocre" testimony, I have always doubted the validity of my faith. Why wasn't I like other people? Why didn't I have that one big moment in my life? Maybe I wasn't truly following God? I know many people would claim that it is wonderful that I have known God my entire life and that I never strayed very far from him, but for a girl with an insecurity about being too quiet and timid, I was never able to accept this as a positive.

Society praises risk-takers and in a similar way, doesn't Christian culture do the same? Don't we relish those testimonies that include a dramatic change? We seem to put more value on those testimonies because we believe they hold more power. They show the radical change that Christ can have in our hearts. Don't get me wrong, these testimonies truly *are* amazing and they *do* have immense power. I am thankful for those who have been far from God and are now living in the freedom of Christ. But what about those who have a different kind of story? Are these stories less than? Are we afraid that if we share a different kind of testimony that it won't have the same impact? I don't know about you, but I've shared this very fear about my own story. Maybe it is time we start placing the same importance on the little moments as we do on the big ones.

These are the little moments that together, become not so little moments. Moment by moment, layer by layer, they have formed the story of my faith.

3

NOT SO LITTLE

It was my sophomore year in college, and I had developed a crush on a college guy who was a few years older. He was kind, respectful and friendly towards me, and I naively interpreted that as something more. After months of being in the "friend zone," I realized that I had been wrong about his feelings toward me. The annual fall retreat was coming up, and I couldn't take it any longer -- I wanted to let him know how I felt so that I could finally move on. I had planned to tell him that weekend, but after feeling the Holy Spirit's prompting to talk to the college director's wife about the situation, I took her advice to let it go. After all, I pretty much knew what his answer was going to be, I just didn't want to admit it to myself.

Later that night, we gathered in the main living area for a worship set. The worship team started playing a song and it was as if my eyes started to tear up the second I heard the melody. It was an older song – one that I had never heard them play before, but knew from my childhood. It was a song my mother used to sing/hum to me when I couldn't fall asleep.

"I love you, Lord and I lift my voice, to worship you, oh my soul, rejoice. Take joy my King, in what you hear. May it be a sweet, sweet sound in your ear."

This song had always been a source of comfort to me, and in my spirit, I knew God had planned it for this very moment. Tears streamed down my face as I realized that God, in his uniquely divine way, was comforting and speaking life to my hurting heart. This was one of the first times that I can remember feeling his presence that intimately.

It was a gorgeous summer day in West Michigan. We had just moved to the area, and I was out for a quick jog. The route I usually took went by a beautiful field – always filled with beautiful little yellow and white butterflies gracefully chasing each other around. Unconsciously, my mind wandered until one little yellow butterfly caught my attention. I immediately thought of one of my dear friends. I always think of her and her sister when I see those little yellow butterflies. Her sister died of cancer when she was young and the same yellow butterflies were flying around at her funeral. Now, whenever my friend sees one, she is reminded of her sister. I continued reflecting as I kept walking on and began thinking about the book that I was reading at the time, called *Beautiful Outlaw* by John Eldredge. He speaks about the little ways in which Jesus tries to interact with us each day. I began to wonder why it was so easy for something as simple as a small butterfly to make me think of a friend, yet Jesus, the Creator of all things, is so hard to recognize in the midst of my daily life. Lost in thought, something caught my eye again. I was past the field, but there was another little butterfly. This one was white. I smiled and laughed. I looked away and there was another one. It seemed as though everywhere I looked, another would appear a few seconds later. In an instant, my heart understood. Jesus was interacting with me in that very moment. Even as I was in the midst of my day, distracted by my own thoughts, Jesus was there, patiently trying to gain my attention.

Fast forward to a few months later, and I was in the midst of job hunting for a full-time job in my career field. I had applied and received an interview with a custom home builder in the area as a design assistant. I was extremely nervous. I had so many butterflies in my stomach (no pun intended). As I drove to the office for my interview, can you guess what flew by my windshield? Yep, you guessed it – a little white butterfly. It was just a quick glimpse, but it flitted right past my line of sight with such grace that I was actually surprised, considering how fast my car was moving. I couldn't hold back my smile. Once again, Jesus was turning my thoughts toward him, showing me that I had nothing to fear. I went into that interview with confidence and left feeling even more confident. A few weeks later, I found out that I got the job. I am still working at that same company to this day. To make things even more incredible, it is owned by an amazing Christian couple who introduced us to the church that my husband and I now call home. It has been above and beyond what I ever could have dreamed possible in a job. But perhaps my favorite part of this story is the moment in which I saw that little white butterfly fly across my windshield. It was another moment that I could distinctly sense God's presence and the unfolding of his perfect will for my life.

It is moments like these that create my story of faith. I could share circumstance after circumstance where I felt God speak to me, shape me and guide me. Most of these moments are small. A song playing at the perfect moment, a show of little white butterflies just for me, a heavenly realization while walking to class. Words that seem to come to life as I'm reading scripture, divine words from a friend or my husband, those "AHA" moments where I finally realize what God is trying to teach me. A quiet conviction from the Holy Spirit, goosebumps during worship, being so inspired that I look down and I've created something so beautiful there is no way I could have done so on my own. Those moments when I desperately need God to come through and in a way that only he can, he provides me with just what I need. These are the little moments that together, become not so little moments. Moment by moment, layer by layer, they have formed the story of my faith. And when you take a good look at it, these little moments aren't little or trivial at all. I've found that my small revelations have consistently laid the foundation for big transformation to take place in my life.

He has given you a story to tell – a story that is necessary and powerful in a way no one else can replicate.

4

ON THE CONTRARY

Maybe you're like me. Maybe you feel like your testimony isn't very special. Maybe you've had a fairly mediocre story. Or maybe at this point you're thinking, *My story is nothing like hers.* Maybe our stories are completely different, but I guarantee we have at least one thing in common: the desire to feel significant and a moment or moments when you have felt completely insignificant.

Regardless of your story, if you've ever felt insignificant in any way, I am here to say:

You are not alone.

Up until about a month ago, I had not been baptized in water as an adult. For those of you who aren't familiar, water baptism is a prophetic act of obedience where we are buried with Christ through baptism in water and raised with Christ to live a new life, free of sin. Growing up in the church, I had plenty of opportunities to get baptized, but I held back. When I was a preteen and they were offering it, I convinced myself that it wasn't for me. I wasn't a bold person. I didn't have that kind of courage. Like I mentioned before, I didn't see this as something I could change. I just accepted it and internalized the shame.

I had a second opportunity as a college student. One of the college girls accepted Jesus while we were on our annual spring break trip. That same spring, the girl who was recently saved and a small group of others decided to get baptized all on the same Sunday. This time, it had been a few years since I had started pursuing God on a deeper level, and it felt like it was too late for me. I was so used to staying in my comfort zone that I let the opportunity pass. What I had missed didn't even occur to me until after the fact.

After that day, I couldn't stop thinking about it. It would randomly enter my thoughts and I would feel the shame creep up on me like a hovering shadow. Seemingly unrelated topics would trigger it. Finally, one day I asked my husband, *"What if I'm not saved because I haven't been baptized?"* I had allowed it to eat me up so much, that I was actually questioning the validity of my own faith. It started to feel like it was this deep, dark secret that nobody knew except me, my husband, my family and a few close friends. The enemy would attack me, and I would start questioning everything.

"Why don't you have a testimony like everyone else?" "If you were truly a Christ follower you would have chosen to be baptized by now." "Maybe if you weren't so quiet and timid, you would be making more of an impact for God."

The shame was so intense that one day I broke down as I was talking with my husband. I realized that not only was I ashamed that I hadn't chosen to be baptized yet, but also that I wasn't bolder in my faith. Deep down, I still felt like "preschool me" – timid and insecure.

A couple weeks later, our campus leader at church asked to meet with us just to get to know us better and talk about what the church believed. I knew he was going to ask about baptism and my stomach did flip-flops thinking about how he would respond to my answer. Would he judge me? Would he think that I wasn't truly saved? What would he say?

We met for lunch a few days later. One of his first questions was about our testimonies. With very little passion, I launched into the boring and simplified rendition of my story and when I finished, I was surprised to hear that he too had accepted Christ at a young age. Immediately, my heart began to slow as I realized that I wasn't the only one with a story like mine. Then he asked the dreaded baptism question...

I hesitated, but then was honest and told him that I had never been baptized in water (other than as a baby). I don't even remember his immediate reaction because I was so nervous. But what I do remember was an absolutely gracious response. There was no judgement. There was no condemnation. All he asked was a simple question, *"Would you like to be baptized?"*

In this moment, I saw God's grace for me. His reaction to an area I was lacking in was not of shame or disgrace, but of invitation and love.

We continued to talk during this meeting about spiritual

gifts and the Holy Spirit. He gave us quite a few scriptures to read that described and discussed these subjects in more depth.

The next morning, I grabbed my Bible and opened up to 1 Corinthians to read the verses he had outlined for us. As I was reading, one chapter really spoke to me. It was 1 Corinthians 12:12-26 (NIV):

Just as a body, though one, has many parts, but all its many parts form one body, so it is with Christ. For we were all baptized by one Spirit so as to form one body – whether Jews or Gentiles, slave or free – and we were all given the one Spirit to drink. Even so the body is not made up of one part but of many.

Now if the foot should say, "Because I am not a hand, I do not belong to the body," it would not for that reason stop being part of the body. And if the ear should say, "Because I am not an eye, I do not belong to the body," it would not for that reason stop being part of the body. If the whole body were an eye, where would the sense of hearing be? If the whole body were an ear, where would the sense of smell be? But in fact,

God has placed the parts of the body, every one of them, just as he wanted them to be. If they were all one part, where would the body be? As it is, there are many parts, but one body.

The eye cannot say to the hand, "I don't need you!" And the head cannot say to the feet, "I don't need you!" On the contrary, those parts of the body that seem to be weaker are indispensable, and the parts that we think are less honorable we treat with special honor. And the parts that are unpresentable are treated with special modesty, while our presentable parts need no special treatment. But God has put the body together, giving greater honor to the parts that lacked it, so that there should be no division in the body, but that its parts should have equal concern for each other. If one part suffers, every part suffers with it; if one part is honored, every part rejoices with it.

On the contrary, the parts that seem to be weaker are *indispensable*.

This word "indispensable" seemed to jump out of the page as I quietly read this passage that morning. Later as I shared the same passage with my husband, he pointed out the exact same line.

The definition of indispensable is simple. It means *absolutely necessary*. God spoke this word over me and my life as I read it in his word that day. Although my story may appear "weaker" according to the world's standards, God assured me it is absolutely necessary within the body of Christ.

This revelation freed me from the cloud of shame I was lost in. I didn't need to be ashamed of myself or my story anymore. I realized that God was lovingly inviting me to take that next step of faith by getting baptized. He was not condemning me because I had failed to take that step, rather he was patiently and expectantly waiting for me to move forward. What Satan was trying to use for evil, God was using for good. It was as though all the obstacles, excuses, fears and anxieties I had created in my head were completely eradicated. I was finally free to move forward in faith and be baptized in water.

That Sunday I was extremely nervous. I'm not a big water person, and I definitely don't like being the center of attention (as you have probably already gathered about me). The idea of getting dunked in front of the entire congregation definitely gave me some anxiety. When the moment finally arrived, I remember feeling such relief as I came up from the water. It was as if this huge weight had been lifted from me. Immediately following was an opportunity for members of my church community to share any prophetic words they received from the Lord (God still speaks today, and he likes to speak to and through us. A prophetic word is meant to edify, encourage and uplift).

A small group gathered around me and began speaking words full of truth, life, and encouragement. I felt overwhelmed with the presence of the Lord as I heard words of promise, potential and affirmation pour from those I knew and those I didn't know. However, it was a word from my newfound friend Lauren, that really hit home.

"God told me that in your gentleness, you are bold. And in your sweetness, you are fierce. And that he is never going to stop calling those things out of you. And that what he's done in your life is significant and that you are going to call others to see their significance. So just know that today God is lighting a fire in your heart to do those things and he's never going to stop calling those out of you."

Tears streamed down my face as this sister in Christ spoke these words over me. God was confirming the word he had spoken over my life just a few weeks earlier. Rather than being called "quiet" and "shy," he was calling me "gentle" and "sweet." Rather than labeling me as "timid" and "unsure," he was declaring me "bold" and "fierce." Rather than having a story of insignificance, he was giving my story significance, and he was calling me to help others see their significance.

Whether you have felt insignificant for only a moment or you've felt it your entire life, God has placed a message on my heart just for you:

You, a precious daughter or son of the King, are irrevocably and unquestionably significant. Your story is absolutely necessary within the body of Christ. He has given you talents, passions, and dreams on purpose and for a purpose. He has given you a story to tell – a story that is necessary and powerful in a way that no one else can replicate. Ephesians 2:10 (TPT) says, *"We have become his poetry, a re-created people that will fulfill the destiny he has given each of us, for we are joined to Jesus, the Anointed One. Even before we were born, God planned in advance our destiny and the good works we would do to fulfill it!"*

When we believe that
we are necessary within
the body of Christ,
we take a seat at the
table instead of choosing
to look on from the
outskirts.

5

ABSOLUTELY NECESSARY

God created the human body to function together in harmony. Each part was created with a unique purpose that helps the body perform as it should. Take away the eyes and you no longer have sight. Take away the stomach and you no longer have digestion. Take away the muscles and you no longer have movement. Each part is necessary for the body to work and function as God created it to.

It is the same with the body of Christ. Each member of the body is unique and has been gifted with specific talents for specific purposes. We cannot say one person's story is more necessary than another because God created each one of us with a unique purpose in mind.

"The eye cannot say to the hand, "I don't need you!" And the head cannot say to the feet, "I don't need you!" On the contrary the parts of the body that seem to be weaker are indispensable, and the parts of the body that we think are less honorable we treat with special honor. And the parts that are unpresentable are treated with special modesty, while our presentable parts need no special treatment. But God has put the body together, giving greater honor to the parts that lacked it, so that there should be no division in the body, but that its parts should have equal concern for each other." 1 Corinthians 12:21-25 (NIV)

Again, the definition of indispensable is *absolutely necessary.* I love how straightforward that is, because God sees it the same. You and your story are absolutely necessary in his Kingdom. There is no doubt or question in the Father's mind. You and your story belong. There is a seat reserved for you at the table and no one else can fill it.

You have a story to tell and a message to give that is invaluable for others to hear. While the work he is doing in your life may feel unnecessary or insignificant at times, God is using it to shape your story and your testimony for his glory and purposes.

Ruth's life is a perfect example of God using what may seem trivial and small to play an invaluable role in his redemptive plan.

Ruth married into the Israelite family of Elimelech and Naomi. Shortly after her father-in-law died, so did her own husband and brother-in-law, leaving her widowed. Naomi instructed her daughters-in-law to go find new husbands, but Ruth refused. Instead, she joined Naomi as they traveled back to her homeland. It was there that she took a lowly job as a gleaner in the fields. This meant that after the fieldworkers harvested the crop, she would come behind and gather the scraps. One day, the owner of the field, Boaz, saw her gleaning and had compassion on her. He asked all his workers to treat her with honor and respect and to make sure that she had gathered enough scraps to sustain her and her mother-in-law. Later, we find out that Boaz is a family relative and after Ruth follows Naomi's advice to approach him, Boaz decides to take Ruth as his wife, becoming the family's guardian redeemer.

To be honest, when I look at Ruth's story from an outsider's perspective, it seems fairly ordinary. Without knowing her inner thought life, prayer life, or her day-to-day interactions with people, it is hard to see the impact that she had.

Essentially, she experienced grief from the death of her husband, decided to follow her mother-in-law instead of getting remarried, and eventually married Boaz. Not a very impactful story when you summarize it into a single sentence. But God knew Ruth's story was valuable. He knew all of her inner thoughts, her prayers, and her day-to-day interactions with people. He knew that she was a faithful daughter. He knew all this when he led her to Boaz and when they had a son named Obed, who had a son named Jesse, who had a son named David, who had a son named Solomon, who had a son named Rehoboam…who had a son named Jacob, who had a son named Joseph, who had a son named JESUS.

God determined from the beginning that Ruth would play an indispensable role in his redemptive plan for us. He deemed her story as absolutely necessary. Despite the fact that it may have seemed insignificant at the time, Ruth's faithfulness in the little things led her to the big things God had for her in his Kingdom – including the role as one of Jesus' foremothers!

How would your perspective change if you actually believed that God viewed your story as important in his Kingdom? Can you imagine how much honor Ruth probably would have felt had she known at the time that she was a foremother of the Messiah? I'm confident she would have been overwhelmed and humbled! Yet she was completely unaware. She had no idea the impact her life was going to have on the future ahead of her.

Friend, what if you just don't realize the seeds that you sow daily?

What if you just don't realize how valuable your opinion and your voice is to those around you?

What if you just don't realize the weight you hold in people's lives?

What if you just don't realize the impact your story is going to have on generations to come?

Aware or not, God is using your story for his glory. When we believe that we are necessary within the body of Christ, we take a seat at the table instead of choosing to stand back and look on from the outskirts. So join me at the table, friend. God is waiting for you to fill your seat so that he can fill you with all that he has for your life.

When we compare
ourselves to others,
we lose sight of God's
specific purpose for
our lives and what
he's called us to do.

6

BEYOND COMPARE

She entered the room with confidence and purpose. Even being late, she was the life of the party in 0.2 seconds. She immediately started chatting with a few girls next to me. I sat there quietly listening in, while working on one of my college projects, as she stole virtually every girl's attention in the room. She made jokes that had every girl laughing and quick-witted remarks flew from her mouth without her even batting an eyelash… safe to say, I was intimidated. She was everything I was not – bold, funny, witty, confident, and charismatic. I tried to play it cool and mind my own business, so I went back to rendering my interior design project and hoped she didn't notice me. I was convinced she wouldn't like me. Why would a girl like her want to be friends with a girl like me? I was quiet, gentle, soft spoken, and sweet…but definitely not sassy. She wouldn't approve.

My thoughts were interrupted as I heard her loudly exclaim, *"WHOA!"* Startled, I looked up to see her staring at my rendering. *"Girl, you drew that?! You are SO talented!! Like seriously, that's amazing. I can't believe you did that all by hand! That's insane. I would be horrible. Absolutely horrible. Like I'm not even kidding you."*

I sat there stunned for a moment. Wait a minute, this girl was actually talking to me? Not only was she talking to me, but she was giving me a compliment! What was happening?!

But there she was smiling at me like we were great friends, even though we hadn't even officially met. We continued to talk and even joke around as the night went on and I couldn't help but think, *"I really like this girl!"*

She didn't know it at the time, but that initial compliment tore down the walls of intimidation that had formed in my mind. It cleared the way for us to genuinely get to know each other.

A year passed, and in that time, we became close friends.

I found that I was not the only one who had been intimidated. Unlike I originally assumed, she had insecurities too. Very much like me, she had felt the world's rejection. When the world was telling me that I wasn't loud enough, the world was telling her that she was too loud. When the world was telling me that I wasn't bold enough, the world was telling her that she was too aggressive. We realized that although we represented two very opposite ends of the spectrum, we could surprisingly relate to each other extremely well.

Comparison is like a thief. It steals our joy, our individuality, and our purpose. When we compare ourselves to others, we lose sight of God's specific purpose for our lives and what he's called us to do. Instead we focus on what he's called another brother or sister to. We fixate on *their* purpose and *their* calling. This can cause jealousy, discontentment and bitterness. Embracing the life that God has called us to live starts with freeing ourselves of comparison.

Let's take a look at a book in the Bible that highlights the story of a woman whose life was beyond comparison. Her name is Esther.

Esther was an orphan who was raised by her uncle, Mordecai, a Jew living in the city of Susa. Her story starts after a turn of events that causes King Ahasuerus to banish his wife, Queen Vashti. After the queen is banished, the king calls for all the beautiful young virgins to be rounded up and put into a rigorous beauty regimen and training program before being presented to him as new heirs to the throne.

I imagine being in Esther's position, it could have been very easy to struggle with comparison. Can you imagine being forced into a group of the most beautiful women in the kingdom just to compete for the king's attention and favor? Although it mentions that Esther was outwardly beautiful, I'm sure she had her insecurities. I can imagine she frequently struggled with comparing herself in more ways than one to the hundreds of other young women in her same position. Yet, we see that she ultimately didn't let this affect God's call on her life.

Esther went on to win the favor of the king and was chosen to be the next queen in place of Queen Vashti. Mordecai had instructed that she not disclose that she was a Jew, so she kept this to herself as she took her new position as queen. After Esther had been appointed to her position, Haman the Agagite, was promoted to be the highest official. The king commanded that all the officials at the king's gate bow down and pay homage to Haman. Being a Jew, Mordecai refused, and it was brought to Haman's attention. Furious, Haman sought to destroy all the Jews throughout the kingdom of Ahasuerus. After a convincing argument to the king, a decree was issued that commanded all officials to kill and destroy the Jews – men, women and children.

When Esther heard of this, she was deeply distressed. Mordecai sent a messenger asking her to beg the king for his favor and plead on behalf of her people. I find Esther's initial response similar to what my own might be in this situation.

"All the king's officials and the people of the royal provinces know that for any man or woman who approaches the king in the inner court without being summoned by the king has but one law: that they be put to death unless the king extends the gold scepter to them and spares their lives. But thirty days have passed since I was called to go to the king." Esther 4:11 (NIV)

Esther's response revealed an uncertainty in herself. Who was she to approach the king? You can tell that she didn't feel fit for the assignment. Have you ever responded to something God has called you to do in a similar way? I know I have. Fortunately, this isn't the end of her story. Mordecai urges her once more, this time reminding her that God has called her to more.

"Do not think that because you are in the king's house you alone of all the Jews will escape. For if you remain silent at this time, relief and deliverance for the Jews will arise from another place, but you and your father's family will perish. **And who knows but that you have come to your royal position for such a time as this?"** *Esther 4:13-14 (NIV)*

God had placed Esther in her position of power for a purpose – to stand up for his people and to deliver them from certain death. She had a choice to make in that moment. Was she going to decide to shrink back and wallow in self-pity, questioning "why me?" or to step out in faith, trusting that the Lord would give her strength and courage? If you've read this story before, you know the answer – after three days of fasting and prayer, Esther approaches the king. When king Ahasuerus sees Esther, he is pleased with her and holds out the golden scepter, sparing her life. She invites both Haman and the king to a banquet that same day. At this banquet, she makes her plea. Upon hearing Esther's request, the king is overcome with compassion for her and her people. He proceeds to write another decree on behalf of all the Jews in his kingdom. This decree not only overturned Haman's original edict, but it gave the Jews the right to protect themselves and to plunder their enemies.

Ultimately, Esther didn't let comparison threaten God's call on her life. Although it could have been an easy trap for her, she chose to courageously follow God's purpose for her and in the process, God used her to save his people.

When thinking of titles for this chapter, I stumbled across the phrase "beyond compare." By definition it means *of a quality or nature surpassing all others of the same kind.* Because God made each person completely and uniquely different, you are not of the "same kind" as your fellow sister or brother. He made you in his unique image. He made you beyond compare.

If the whole body were an eye, where would the sense of hearing be? If the whole body were an ear, where would the sense of smell be? But in fact, God has placed the parts of the body, every one of them, just as he wanted them to be. If they were all one part, where would the body be? 1 Corinthians 12:17-19 (NIV)

God did not create you to be what you are not or to live in a constant state of comparison. As Paul explains in this passage, he has created each person *"as he wanted them to be."*

Just as each part of the human body is unique – so are you. One form of the definition of "compare" is *to be of equal or similar nature or quality*. Your story is not of a similar nature to any other, therefore, it can't be compared. God did not create us to love us equally, but to love us uniquely.

It is only when we
undoubtedly know
our significance
that we can effectively
call others to theirs.

7

SMALL BUT SIGNIFICANT

As I mentioned in the preface, hummingbirds are the perfect example of incredible power and significance wrapped in a small package. They may appear delicate and trivial, but they are quite the opposite. God created hummingbirds to be remarkably powerful and to play a role that is extremely necessary and important.

The small, the tiny, the little — God sees it all as significant. He puts importance on the details. He is not an absent-minded God. He created each and every detail of this beautiful earth mindfully and purposefully. We can be certain that he sees, knows and cares, and that he has given each of our stories significance. Luke 12:6-7 (MSG) says, *"What's the price of two or three pet canaries? Some loose change, right? But God never overlooks a single one. And he pays even greater attention to you, down to the last detail — even numbering the hairs on your head! So don't be intimidated by all this bully talk. You're worth more than a million canaries."*

As I was praying over this chapter, I felt God stir in my spirit a call to those of you who have felt *lost, forgotten, or like an outcast* out of hiding and into his glorious light and love.

TO THOSE WHO HAVE FELT LOST

Have you ever been lost before? In those moments, there is a sense of panic and helplessness. Everything is unfamiliar and you could be so close to your destination, but because you don't know your surroundings, you don't know how to get where you need to be. The same can happen when we feel lost spiritually. We may be so close to the truth of our identity in Christ, but we can't grab ahold of it until the truth becomes our reality.

God's desire for the lost is that they know the truth and that they are found in him. In Luke 15:1-7 (NIV), Jesus makes known God's heart for the lost:

"Now the tax collectors and sinners were all gathering around to hear Jesus. But the Pharisees and the teachers of the law muttered, 'This man welcomes sinners and eats with them.'

Then Jesus told them this parable: "Suppose one of you has a hundred sheep and loses one of them. Doesn't he leave the ninety-nine in the open country and go after the lost sheep until he finds it? And when he finds it, he joyfully puts it on his shoulders and goes home. Then he calls his friends and neighbors together and says, 'Rejoice with me; I have found my lost sheep.' I tell you that in the same way there will be more rejoicing in heaven over one sinner who repents than over ninety-nine righteous persons who do not need to repent."

Have you heard the disapproving mutters of the Pharisees? Maybe you have sensed others' disdain and felt ashamed of your story. It is easy to feel "inferior" in Christian communities where religion is greater than relationship, e≠specially if your story has been a fairly colorful one. Maybe you feel unfit or unqualified? Maybe you carry a lot of shame from your past mistakes? Whatever it is that is making you feel like a lost sheep, hear this about God: He is a GOOD Shepherd. He will go after *the one* lost sheep. When he finds it, he will rejoice over it more than all the others. He gives honor and celebrates those who are found in him. If there was no worth attributed to a single lost sheep, then the Shepherd would cut his loss and stay with the rest of his herd. Yet, this isn't the parable that Jesus tells the Pharisees. The Shepherd goes out in pursuit of the lost sheep, giving significance even to the one who went astray.

When others call you unfit, unqualified, or unworthy because of your past – God calls you significant. He has a heart for the lost and a place for you in his herd. So, whether you feel lost or have felt lost in the past – know that your identity in Christ is just around the corner, waiting for you to grab hold of it. He wants to remove your shame, give you honor and use your story for his glory.

TO THOSE WHO HAVE FELT FORGOTTEN

Have you ever had anyone forget your birthday? What about forget the plans that you had with them? It's easy in these moments to feel like they forgot more than your birthday or your plans. It feels more like they forgot *you*.

These moments can often make us feel insignificant and unimportant. If they cared, they would remember, right? Unfortunately, because no one is perfect, even our close friends and family will fail us. The good news is that even when those we love disappoint or forget us, our identity in Christ doesn't change. He has not forgotten us. He still sees us and deems us significant.

Starting in Luke 8:40, Jesus is greeted by a crowd of people. A man named Jairus, a ruler of the synagogue, approaches Jesus and begs him to come to his house to heal his daughter. Jesus has compassion on him and begins to make his way to this leader's house. As he is going there, a woman who had been bleeding for twelve years, reaches out and barely touches the edge of his cloak.

Now let's pause for a moment. This woman had been bleeding for *twelve years!* The Bible tells us that she had spent all her money on doctors who could not heal her, leaving her poor and probably dressed in nothing but rags. Not to mention, during this time, women were considered "unclean" during any type of bleeding. This woman had been considered "unclean" for twelve years. I can imagine that the community had forgotten and given up on her as they figured that she could not be healed. But despite all this, she reached out to touch the edge of Jesus' cloak, believing as she did, that she would be healed. Luke 8:44-48 (NIV) describes what happens after she reaches out in faith.

"She came up behind him and touched the edge of his garment, and immediately her bleeding stopped. 'Who touched me?' Jesus asked. When they all denied it, Peter said, 'Master, the people are crowding and pressing against you.' But Jesus said, 'Someone touched me; I know that power has gone out from me.' Then the woman, seeing that she could not go unnoticed, came trembling and fell at his feet. In the presence of all the people, she told why she had touched him and how she had been instantly healed. Then he said to her, 'Daughter, your faith has healed you. Go in peace.'"

What an amazing story, right? While the healing power that Jesus exhibits and the tremendous faith of this woman is quite breathtaking – I think there is more to glean from this story than a simple lesson of faith and breakthrough. This woman is a woman who is unnamed, unclean, and unnoticed. In the eyes of her community, she is essentially forgettable. Jairus, on the other hand, is a synagogue leader. He is a prominent member in the community. It is during Jesus' way to heal Jairus' daughter, that he stops to acknowledge this woman. Jesus asks the crowd, *"Who touched me?"* Peter tries to move him along, but Jesus refuses to keep going until he acknowledges the one who went unnoticed.

I believe Jesus chose to stop at this very moment for a reason. He is on the way to heal a very important leader's daughter, yet he stops to take the time to acknowledge and call out an otherwise forgotten woman. Jesus didn't just ignore the touch and think, *"I already know who touched me. This woman can wait. She got what she wanted – she was healed. I have more important things to do..."* and keep going on his way. No. He chose to pause and give his attention to this woman, even though he already knew her name. With this action, Jesus chose to communicate a far deeper message than just exposing the woman. He chose to communicate God's heart for the forgotten.

I know the pain of being forgotten or unnoticed. I've been there. It hurts. But Jesus has been calling you – just as he did the woman in the crowd – out of hiding and into significance.

To Those Who Have Felt Like An Outcast

Have you ever been in a group of people and felt totally out of place? Maybe everyone else had something in common but you? Maybe you've experienced the pain of being left out or uninvited. If you've ever felt "different," than what the world says is "normal" then you've felt like an outcast. The definition of an outcast is *a person who has been rejected by society or a social group.* If any part of that definition seems to ring true for you, God wants to redefine your story.

Whatever qualities the world has told you are unacceptable, unlovable, or unimportant are the very qualities that God loves and cherishes about you. He made you that way for a reason. Jesus displayed the Father's heart for the outcast by spending time with those who had been rejected by society. Throughout his ministry, we see Jesus spending time with tax collectors, prostitutes and lepers. Let's dig into a story about Zacchaeus, a tax collector, whom Jesus becomes very fond of.

> *"Jesus entered Jericho and was passing through. A man was there by the name of Zacchaeus; he was a chief tax collector and was wealthy. He wanted to see who Jesus was, but because he was short he could not see over the crowd. So he ran ahead and climbed a sycamore-fig tree to see him, since Jesus was coming that way.*
>
> *When Jesus reached the spot, he looked up and said to him,*

"Zacchaeus, come down immediately. I must stay at your house today." So he came down at once and welcomed him gladly.

All the people saw this and began to mutter, "He has gone to be the guest of a sinner."

But Zacchaeus stood up and said to the Lord, "Look, Lord! Here and now I give half of my possessions to the poor, and if I cheated anybody out of anything, I will pay back four times the amount."

Jesus said to him, "Today salvation has come to this house, because this man, too, is a son of Abraham."
Luke 19:1-9 (NIV)

Zacchaeus was rejected by society. As a tax collector, he was disliked, even hated, by the rest of the world. He was seen as a sinner and was outcast because of it. That's why when Jesus called to Zacchaeus to come down from the tree so that he could visit with him, the people were appalled. Why would Jesus associate himself with such a man? He was considered "sinful" and his profession was unacceptable, yet Jesus still called him into relationship.

Hear me when I say this: the mutters of the world hold no weight compared to the declarations of Jesus. Jesus declares significance over every person who has ever felt like an outcast. He declares significance over every heart that has ever felt rejected. In the story, Jesus declares that *"this man, too, is a son of Abraham."* This means that the promises God gave to Abraham hold true for Zacchaeus and they hold true for you, too! You are one of God's children – immensely loved and forever cherished. You are not an outcast in the Kingdom of God. Your identity rests solely on who God says you are, and he has called you one of his own. The enemy may continue to make you feel on the outskirts, but regardless of what others say, you can be confident that he calls you his son or daughter. As a son or daughter of the King – you also are an heir to his promises and can expect God's favor over your life.

If one thing is clear to me from the way that Jesus treats people, it's that he gives significance to the insignificant. The definition of "significant" is *sufficiently great or important to be worthy of attention; noteworthy*. Jesus wants you to know that you are worthy of attention. Just as he goes out in pursuit of the one lost sheep or as he took notice of the woman who touched his cloak, or how he called Zacchaeus, the outcast, into a relationship with him – he pursues you too. He wants you to know your significance and to live from a place full of his abundant love.

So, let's dare to believe that what he says about us is true. It is only when we undoubtedly know our significance that we can effectively call others to theirs.

When we are vulnerable and honest with ourselves and others about our insecurities, it is like flipping a light switch or lighting a match. The big shadows of comparison are washed out in the brightness of the Lord's light.

8

OVERCOMING THE SHADOWS

Now that we know where we stand in this search for significance, how do we overcome the deceiving shadows of comparison? How do we move past the lies that tell us if we only looked like her, if we only had his testimony, if we only had her talent, that we would be enough?

I'd like to share three ways I have learned to conquer comparison with the help of my Heavenly Father. By no means are these the only solutions, but they will provide you with some key tools to begin removing the shadows and start walking in God's truth and light.

SHINE A LIGHT ON IT

Remember that friend I described in the opening of chapter 6? Before getting to know her better, I thought I knew all girls like her. To be honest, I assumed that she didn't have any insecurities and that she was totally confident in who she was. But as we have grown closer over the past few years, I've realized that this just isn't the case. As she slowly peeled back the layers of her tough exterior, I realized that she too had insecurities very similar to my own. Ironically, I was actually the epitome of what she felt she needed to be – more quiet, gentle and sweet.

That's just it, friend. Comparison is like trying to see in the dark. When we're in it, we can't see very well, so we create our own ideas about what is lurking in the shadows. A shadow in the dark may appear alive and scary, but in the light, it is just a harmless, inanimate object. When we are vulnerable and honest with ourselves and others about our insecurities, it is like flipping the light switch or lighting a match. The big shadows of comparison are washed out in the brightness of the Lord's light, and the lies that seemed so real are uncovered and seen for what they actually are - silly and unrealistic.

Finding out that my friend actually felt insecure about the very qualities that I longed to have and vice versa released both of us from the enemy's grip. We realized that it wasn't an "us vs. them" issue, but that there was actually more at play. Ephesians 6:12 (NIV) reminds us:

> *"For our struggle is not against flesh and blood, but against the rulers, against the authorities, against the powers of this dark world and against the spiritual forces of evil in the heavenly realms."*

The enemy likes to turn us against each other, and what a more effective way to do that than to use comparison? But when we are transparent and open with each other, the enemy no longer has a foothold. We are free to love without restraints. So, let's shine a light on our insecurities, because I guarantee that when we do, we will find that we aren't so different from each other after all.

SPEAK TRUTH

It might be easy to just stop at that first step – to just expose our insecurities and then move on with life. But trust me when I say, you can't stop there! If anyone has been guilty of releasing insecurities and then just moving on, it's me. For most of my life, this was my pattern. Get them out in the open and then go about my life… until they came barreling right back months, days, or even hours later. It isn't enough to just speak out the lies; we must go a step further and *declare the truth* with our mouths.

Whether you know the Word of God by heart or you've never picked up the Bible, I urge you to get in this holy book. Let it soak in. Let the truth occupy your heart. *"For the word of God is alive and active. Sharper than any double-edged sword, it penetrates even to dividing soul and spirit, joints and marrow; it judges the thoughts and attitudes of the heart."* Hebrews 4:12 (NIV). God's words are not only words, they are living and active! When we speak his truth over ourselves, *out loud*, the atmosphere shifts. Spoken truth has power over the enemy. He can't hear our thoughts, but when we physically move our mouths to truth, he has to flee. At the very least, speak the name of Jesus and the enemy's power will immediately disintegrate.

I feel the need to share with you that this is not something I'm preaching to you from up on a soap box. I am not a master at this practice. This is still something I'm in the process of learning. In fact, I just had to practice this earlier this morning before starting to write this section. God's timing is perfect, isn't it?

The other night I was spending some time with some friends from church. As we sat outside on the back patio, I listened to one of the girls, whom I had never met before, talk about her testimony. As she finished up, another girl mentioned how she loves total transformation stories and how they spur her on in her own faith.

I sat there and listened to her continue on about her own transformation with God and felt the familiar shame creep back up. Now, let me make something clear. I know the girl who made the comment about total transformation was not intending to hurt me or to make me feel ashamed of my own story. She was simply expressing her passion and joy in God. But in that moment of insecurity, I allowed her comment to give the enemy permission to start whispering again. All the familiar lies started flooding back:

"Why don't you have a testimony like everyone else?" "What's wrong with you?" "Maybe if your story wasn't so uneventful you would be making more of an impact for God."

I went home that night feeling beaten up by the enemy and

my own thoughts. My husband asked me what was wrong, and I told him about the war that was raging in my mind. It helped to put words to what I was feeling, as I realized that this was just another attack from the enemy. Even so, I continued to sit in my shame for the rest of the night. Finally, after not being able to fall asleep for an hour, I grabbed my Bible and opened up to 1 Corinthians 12 and read through it again.

"…On the contrary, the parts of the body that seem to be weaker are indispensable…"

I let the words sink in, and I started to feel all the shame leave. I began to feel God's peace permeate my heart again. Shortly after that, I was able to fall asleep.

The next morning, I was at a small group with a few other women. The first thing my small group leader mentioned was how the enemy had been on high "attack mode" over the past week. The first thing she wanted us to do was to go around the group and declare victory over those areas where Satan was trying to steal our joy and peace. When it came to my turn, I told the group what had happened the night before and how Satan had tried to use it for evil. Then I was able to practice speaking out the truth. As I claimed victory in Jesus, I felt a freedom and peace flow through me. I spoke these words:

*"My story **is** needed. My story **is** enough, and it **will** make an impact."*

So, I urge you – seek God in the midst of the lies and let him renew your mind with truth. Look to the Bible, listen to the Holy Spirit and in his perfect way, he will transform your thoughts. Then in confidence, physically *speak out* his truth. Proverbs 18:21 (MSG) says, *"Words kill, words give life; they're either poison or fruit – you choose."* When we choose to speak words of life over our situation or our thoughts, it dramatically shifts the atmosphere around us.

START ENCOURAGING OTHERS

When we have the revelation that we are fearfully and wonderfully made and that we are indispensable in the body of Christ, we are able to see that God created each and every person with their own unique personality and story. Comparison is no longer relevant, because we realize that we are beyond compare.

So, what better way to combat comparison than to do just the opposite? Start encouraging. There's no better antidote than to see another's unique strengths and to empower them to live them out. When we encourage others, we enable courage in one another by giving each other confidence to embrace ourselves as God created us. We were made to encourage, and I can't help but think that when we fail to encourage each other – comparison starts to take root.

If we were all plants, each person would represent a unique species. Each one is different, but all beautiful and important in their own way. When we encourage one another, we must be looking for these subtle, yet distinct, differences that give each of us something unique to bring to the table. The body of Christ is full of men and women who have incomparable stories. What good would it do if we all had similar testimonies? If we were all eyes, where would our hearing be? And if we were all ears, where would our sense of smell be? The body of Christ is only the body of Christ with every part of the body present and contributing. We can only function our best if all the parts are working together in their own unique way.

God has placed encouragement in our lives as a tool to uproot the weeds of comparison. Let's practice spotting the weeds and plucking them out before they start to overtake our gardens. We can't get lazy about encouragement. It isn't something God calls us to do only on our good days. Ephesians 4:29 (TPT) says, *"And never let ugly or hateful words come out of your mouth, but instead let your words become beautiful gifts that encourage others; do this by speaking words of grace that help them."* God created us to live in community, and he did that with the intention that we would speak words of truth and grace to one another. When we truly encourage one another with love, we leave no room for comparison to reside.

Most of the time the message that we received in these past memories can point us to the root of the lie we believe about ourselves in the present.

9

"SPECK OF DIRT" MOMENTS

I sat there as the weight of what I was told moments ago finally began to sink in. I felt paralyzed as the pain began to course through my veins like sharp daggers. *How could this get any worse?* I thought. I looked up from the floor and met the eyes of my friends. Their sympathetic looks made me feel so exposed – *They knew! They knew this whole time! How was I the last to know?*

That memory is so ingrained in my mind, because one moment alone has never made me feel more insignificant. My first boyfriend had broken up with me less than a week ago, and I was completely devastated. My friends sat me down for an "intervention" of sorts, because they knew something I didn't. They knew the real reason he had broken up with me. The truth was that he had been cheating on me with another girl. That girl was a friend of mine and a fellow teammate from the track team. As you can imagine, this news was extremely painful to hear, especially coming from friends and not from either of the parties involved. I had been betrayed by my boyfriend and my friend and neither of them had considered me worth the truth.

Have you ever felt so small that you felt like a speck of dirt? This was my "speck of dirt" moment. I couldn't stop wondering why. *Why hadn't he considered me when he chose to cheat on me? Why hadn't he considered telling me the truth? Why hadn't she considered how much she would hurt me? Why hadn't my friends considered telling me sooner? Why? Why hadn't anyone thought of me?*

If the memory I shared in the first chapter of my classmates pushing me to say something had felt like a *command* to prove my *significance*, this moment felt like a *confirmation* of my *insignificance*.

Insignificance is described in the dictionary as the *quality of being too small or unimportant to be worth consideration.* As we discussed earlier, if you have felt lost, forgotten, or like an outcast, etc., you have felt the sting of insignificance. I believe we have all felt too unimportant to be worth consideration at some point in our lives. Some of you may be able to recall those "speck of dirt" moments more easily, whereas others may have buried those memories so deep that they are completely numb to the pain. Regardless of how far you have to dig, I passionately believe that God is waiting for you to bring these memories to the surface – lay them at the foot of the cross, and then watch him create beauty from ashes.

So how do we go about digging up these "speck of dirt" moments? For some of us, it might only take a moment to recall, but for many of us – it might take some time of reflection. There is no one fix-all method for this, but I would like to discuss a few questions that I believe will help us uncover these moments, find the root and let God be the good gardener that he is.

"WHAT ARE MY MOMENTS ?"

First and foremost, I believe that we must seek God in this. Go ahead – ask the Holy Spirit to reveal those moments to you. Maybe some of them come to mind easily, but there are very likely other memories stored somewhere deep within you that you have repressed and tried to forget because of the pain. Don't be afraid to ask the Lord to reveal the moments in your life when you have felt insignificant. You might be surprised at what he brings to mind.

I've found the best atmosphere for this is in a quiet place. This could be somewhere in your home, at a park, at the beach – wherever you feel most like you can hear the Lord's voice. Once you are all settled in, ask God to bring these "speck of dirt" moments to mind. You might start praying something like this:

> *Father,*
>
> *Please do what you do best and dig up the bad roots in my garden. I know there is a place that my feeling of insignificance stems from and I invite you to bring it to my attention. I know that feeling (insert lost, forgotten, like an outcast, etc.) is not my identity. I am your son or daughter and you give me significance. As you bring painful memories to the forefront, fill me with your comfort and peace.*

After you pray this, give yourself some time to just sit and be. It is hard for us to hear God when we are constantly going from one thing to the next. Let yourself ponder what he might be speaking to you. Trust the memories that he takes you to. They may not seem related at first, but I've found there is always something deeper.

The story I shared at the very beginning of this book was one of those memories for me. As I told you before, I always told that story as a joke -- so when the Lord brought it to mind, I thought, *No. That wasn't a big deal. It was just an awkward moment in my childhood.* But the longer I reflected on it, the more I realized that God was revealing this as one of my "speck of dirt" moments. I had just buried that feeling of insignificance so deep that I didn't associate it with the memory anymore. That being said, it very well may be a memory or memories that you've remembered for a long time, but just didn't know the depth to which they affected you.

"WHAT'S THE ROOT?"

After God has revealed that memory or memories to you, ask him to help you relive it. Now hold on, you're probably thinking, *Is this girl crazy? She's asking me to relive a moment where I felt like a literal speck of dirt?! No way!* Let me clarify.

Yes, I am asking you to relive a painful memory, but I'm not asking you to go through it in your own strength. Ask your loving Father to lead you. He will give you peace and comfort as you navigate your way through feelings like shame, hurt, insignificance, guilt, bitterness, resentment, vulnerability and so much more.

As the Lord gives you courage and you wade through these emotions with him as your strength, ask the Holy Spirit to reveal your bad roots. What is the root of that feeling of insignificance? For me, it was a sense of never being enough. Not being loud enough, outgoing enough, strong enough, brave enough. I had so much shame in simply who I was. A lot of this traced back to one of my very first memories in school.

If you are struggling to get right to the root, ask yourself what kind of feelings does this memory bring up for me? What messages (or lies) did it send me about my identity? Maybe you felt needy or like an inconvenience. Maybe you felt like you were a mistake. Maybe you got the sense that you might be obnoxious or annoying to someone and you internalized that as a truth about yourself. Whatever it is that you felt, press into it and let the Holy Spirit dig deeper. Most of the time the message that we received in these past memories can point us to the root of the lie that we believe about ourselves in the present.

"WHAT WAS JESUS DOING?"

Here comes the crucial part that you don't want to miss in this process. Ask the Lord to show you where Jesus was in the memory he revealed to you. Many times, we feel that God was absent in our moments of insignificance or pain, but if we just ask and look with heavenly eyes -- we will find that Jesus was and is *always* present in these moments. He never leaves us nor forsakes us (Deuteronomy 31:8).

As you are reliving your "speck of dirt" moment, ask the Holy Spirit:

"What was Jesus doing?"

If you ask, I am confident that God will give you an image or words within that moment of your memory. I'd like to share the image that God gave me in my moment of insignificance. First, let me recap that memory:

I was on a field trip with my preschool class and we were at a local park playing on a playground. I don't remember much of what happened before this, but I can clearly remember being surrounded by my classmates. They were all staring at me. After a few moments, one little boy broke the silence and commanded, "Heidi, say something." I whimpered a small, "Hi" and everyone gasped. "She speaks!" they all exclaimed. I hung my head in embarrassment as they kept marveling over the realization that I wasn't, in fact, mute.

I can distinctly remember hanging my head in shame and embarrassment that day. That's why it was so powerful when the Lord showed me an image of Jesus kneeling and lifting my face in his hands. Looking me in the eye with compassion and love, I saw him saying:

"You are my daughter. You are significant. This moment does not define you. Don't look down – look to me. Keep your eyes on my face, and I will show you just how loved, cherished, and significant you truly are."

So, what's your "speck of dirt" moment? And what was Jesus doing in it? Remember that he has never left you. He was there with you in your darkest moment. Let him show you his heart for you as you seek him in the midst of the pain.

Whatever your sphere of influence, you can be confident that God has placed a boldness inside of you to share the message he has given you for such a time as this.

10

LOUDNESS ≠ BOLDNESS

I've never been a "bold" person. As you now know, I was too afraid to ask my teacher to go to the bathroom in preschool. The thought of approaching a stranger on the street, even just to introduce myself is pretty unnerving. I am uncomfortable taking risks, and I prefer to play it safe so I'm confident of the outcome. I rarely change my hairstyle for fear that I won't like it, and I'm definitely not one to make a bet.

I always thought that being bold just wasn't in me. I grew up thinking that it just wasn't my personality and that it was a weakness within myself. This has always been a sensitive area for me, because I've never felt I could measure up to others. Hearing the word "bold," made me feel insignificant. Instead of feeling empowered, I felt ashamed. Reading a verse that described the righteous as being "bold as a lion" made me feel like a failure. Increasingly, I noticed myself develop an insecurity about my testimony. The more bold, risky, transformative testimonies I heard from others – the more insignificant I felt my own story was. It paled in comparison. What bold things had I done for the Lord? Shame taunted me with this unanswered question.

Hear me when I say this: God does not play shame's game. He is a shame slayer, not a shame player.

Many times, when I feel shame over something that the Lord is calling me to, it is because I have formulated my own false definition of what that means. When I felt shame over boldness, I was feeling shame over my false definition of boldness. I thought bold meant only being outgoing. I thought bold meant being blunt and insensitive to others. I thought it meant being loud and opinionated. I thought it meant always causing conflict instead of creating peace. Someone who has an outgoing personality might be bold, but not all who are bold have outgoing personalities. Bold is not a personality trait. It is a trait of the Holy Spirit. God doesn't show boldness, he IS boldness. As a daughter or son of the King, we have that boldness inside of us. It is not of our own personality or our own strength, but it comes from the Holy Spirit. It is a part of our DNA. The good news? We can access it at any time.

"For God has not given us a spirit of fear and timidity, but of power, love, and self-discipline." 2 Timothy 1:7 (NLT)

God has been slowly redefining my definition of boldness. As he always does, he is broadening my view. Just as God can't fit into a neat little box, neither can his definition of boldness. If God calls us all to be "bold as lions" and we are all different, how can there be only one way to act in boldness? We are all individuals with unique personalities, quirks and strengths. Each of our expressions of who the Father is will come with a unique perspective and in a unique way.

I recently received a prophetic word from my friend, Hannah. She said that as I was sharing with the group about this book, she heard God speak the word "roar." She described that normally when we hear the word "roar" we think "loud," but that roars don't always have to be loud. God is showing me that he's given me a "roar" that is powerful and will be full of impact and yet I don't necessarily have to be physically loud to share it. He's given me a story to tell that will give him glory in its own unique way.

Whatever it is that God is calling you to – I encourage you to act in the boldness of who he created you to be. Let's be bold in our gentleness, fierce in our sweetness, daring in our compassion and fearless in our love. He's given you a "roar" to share with the world. Don't discredit yours just because it doesn't sound the same. Whether you have a loud personality or you are quiet like I am, God has a purpose for you. Frequently he chooses the unqualified, the unpopular and the undervalued to do his most remarkable work. Whatever your sphere of influence, you can be confident that God has placed a boldness inside of you to share the message that he has given you for such a time as this.

So what's your "roar?"
What is it that God
has put inside of
you that rages like
a fire?

11

WHAT'S YOUR "ROAR?"

God gives each of us a "roar" to share with the world. One definition of "roar" is a *full, deep, prolonged cry.* God *knows* the cry of our hearts like the back of his hand. He knows them because he placed them there. Those passions and desires inside of us were given to us for a purpose. He wants us to know that he made us indispensable. Our stories have a purpose and he wants to use them to bring others to him.

So, what's your "roar?" What is it that God has put inside of you that rages like a fire? What makes your passion swell? What do you want to be known for? What is the cry of your heart?

If you were to ask me these questions about a year ago, I wouldn't have had a clue how to answer. Sure, I had passions but none seemed to revolve around one message. Then I had the revelation about my own testimony and heard the prophetic words from my sister in Christ: *"...and you are going to call others to see their significance."* After hearing these words, it became quite clear to me.

My "roar" is this:

Encouraging others in the truth that their story holds an indispensable and significant role in the body of Christ.

All my passions relate back to this central theme, this idea that God has created each of us with unique stories, passions, gifts and talents for a specific purpose. They were all given to reflect who he is to the world. You hold a unique reflection of the incomparable God of the universe. Just as there is no one like him, there is also no one like you, as you were created in his image. How amazing is that? No one has ever or will ever express God's love in the way that you do. It is completely unique to who he has created you to be. What freedom there is in knowing that you don't have to compare, compete or strive. You are exactly the way you were meant to be! When we embrace that freedom, and we embrace our stories in light of who we are, we are living the lives that our Father intended us to live.

To all of you who are reading this and still don't have a clue what your "roar" is, I encourage you to do two things: ask God what he says about you and ask him how he wants to use your story.

EMBRACING YOU

It was a Friday night, and we were sitting across from each other in my college apartment. Both of us had our homework sprawled across the table. My laptop was playing my favorite playlist. We worked a little, talked a little and stole a few admiring glances at one another every so often. It was those early days in the relationship when doing something together even as boring as homework felt magical.

The song changed to one of my current favorites at the time – an upbeat, happy song. It was one of those songs that made me feel like I couldn't help but dance. I jumped to my feet and declared that I was going to take a little dance break. He looked up at me with surprised, but excited eyes. *"You can't watch me!"* I commanded him, feeling like a bashful little girl.

With a grin on his face, he promised not to watch. Feeling safe, I danced away until my heart was content. Little did I know, he was watching me the entire time. Toward the end of the song, I noticed his gaze and my dance moves slowed. *"Hey! I said no looking!"* I squealed, embarrassed. That's when I saw his huge smile and the look in his eyes said it all. *"You are so adorable,"* he told me. I avoided his gaze as I sat down at the table and tried to hide the smile that was slowly forming on my lips.

When I think back to the times where I have felt the most free to be myself, this is one of those rare moments. My boyfriend at the time (now my husband) probably didn't even realize how powerful this moment was to me. His reaction to my crazy, weird and hyper dance moves was one of the many things that proved he was the one. He made me feel like I could be 100% myself without any fear. Even when I wasn't sure that I could embrace who I truly was, he saw and embraced me. That moment dancing around like a crazy person in my college apartment without any inhibitions is a moment I remember feeling so free to just be me. I was who I was, and my husband's response was one of delight.

Those rare moments where you are just being you, are the very moments God is absolutely delighted with you. He looks at you with a huge grin on his face. His response to you embracing who you are is not one of rejection or disappointment, but of pure joy. Nothing makes the Father's heart happier than seeing his children be who he created them to be. Just as my husband's response was one of admiration and love, so is our Heavenly Father's. We can be sure that he sees us – all of us – and that he loves what he sees.

Those weird, quirky, unlikeable, unpopular, odd, uncommon, dorky qualities about you are the very things that God cherishes. He wants you to embrace those things as beautiful because he made you without flaw. Song of Solomon 4:7 (ESV) says, *"You are altogether beautiful, my love; there is no flaw in you."* Those qualities you try to hide or wish away are meant to be there. Embrace them. He calls them beautiful.

So, what are those rare moments for you? The moments when you have felt free to be you without any boundaries, limits, or worries? These are the moments that we must let God speak to us in. When we listen to what he says about us in these moments, we will begin to see ourselves the way that he sees us and value ourselves the way that he values us.

LETTING HIM USE YOUR STORY

Our stories are very much intertwined with who we think we are and how we interact with the world. They hold all of our experiences, relationships, successes, failures, hopes, dreams, ideas and thoughts. They give others a glimpse into how we have developed into the person that we are today. Our stories hold power. They give meaning and add depth to a person. They reveal the ways that God has moved and is moving in our lives. When we share our testimonies, we strengthen the faith of those around us.

I think it is vital to not only share our stories, but to know why they are important. God has a beautiful way of weaving his character into each and every person's testimony. Maybe your story shows his redemptive love for us, his gentle pursuit of us, his explosive grace for us, or his never-ending faithfulness to us. Whatever it is, there is something about your story that speaks to who God is and to who he is revealed through you.

Earlier I mentioned that I had an opportunity to get baptized in college but didn't take it. I remember sitting there at the service with some of my closest friends and watching their testimony videos play up on the screen. As I watched and listened to each of them tell their story, I began to feel insecure. Each of these wonderful friends of mine had such an amazing testimony of how God's grace had impacted them and how he had pursued them even in the midst of them being lost. I couldn't help but think about my own story and how it had been pretty uneventful up to that point in my life. I never had a falling out with God. The closest I got to turning away from him was in high school when I had been dating a guy who was not pursuing God and who didn't have the same morals as I did. Even then, I never walked away from my faith. I flirted with fire, but I never went up in flames. Part of me almost wished I had, because then I could have had a story like these friends of mine, one that made God's presence feel undeniable. My testimony felt like a story plot that had the potential to be really good, but just fell flat in the end and left you feeling disappointed. After wrestling with this on my own for awhile, I finally turned to God to see what he had to say about it.

And here's what God showed me: while my story might not be the most apparent example of God's explosive grace for us, it is a beautiful example of *his faithfulness* to us. Despite the pressure to conform to this world, I haven't fallen off course. All my life, I've known God's goodness. I've known his love. I've known his grace. I've known his favor and provision. I've known his peace and joy. There is significance in that.

I once heard a sermon from one of the campus leaders at our church and she said this, "God is a God of the mountaintops AND the valleys." I wholeheartedly believe this to be true. The same God who is full of transformation, restoration, and radical change is also a God who is steadfast, consistent and faithful. I can attest to this from my own personal story. God exemplifies both of these qualities equally. His power is evident in both the mountaintops and the valleys.

So, I challenge you to ask him what he says about your story. What quality of his is on display when you tell it? What piece of his character has he skillfully woven into the fibers of your testimony?

Just let those questions linger in that sacred space between you and Jesus. It might not come to you right away or tomorrow or the next day. It might take a week or maybe a month or more for you to fully understand the treasure that

he has bestowed you with. But I promise you – it's there and
he is patiently waiting for you to discover it.

I pray that you would know the depth to which he deems your story indispensable and that you would tell it with boldness, expecting God to use it in bigger ways than you could ever imagine.

12

THIS IS FOR YOU

My goal in writing this book has never been just about me. I didn't decide to write this to say, *"Hey everyone, LOOK, I can write a book!"* This has always been about the call I heard on my life through those prophetic words that were spoken over me at my baptism. They were a calling to call others to see their significance. I want this book to be more than just beautifully written words on a page; I want these words to be filled with the Holy Spirit's presence. I want you to be drawn closer to who God is and to who he has created you to be. I hope that by giving you a raw and vulnerable look into my struggles, my story, and my life, you have learned more about your own story and who God has created you to be. But most importantly, I want you to walk away after having read this and to know without a doubt that YOUR unique story is absolutely necessary within the body of Christ.

I know that I have the tendency to say, *"Well that's great for her/him… but I'm a different story."* For those of you who might be thinking that right now, I'd like to speak into that by saying YES – you ARE a different story and that's OKAY. But this truth that we are each unique, significant, and necessary is not just for me or your fellow brothers and sisters in Christ. This message is for you, too!

I was struggling with how to wrap up the end of this book, because there were so many different directions I could go with it. Do I summarize what I said in previous chapters? Do I end with a big challenge? Do I leave them with a manifesto of sorts? What's going to give them just what they need to move forward? Ultimately, I landed on sharing a few stories from some of the most influential women in my life. In this final chapter, I am going to quickly, but distinctly shine a light on four different stories of four different women and have them share what their "roar" is. Like I mentioned earlier, there is power when we share our testimony. Read through these women's stories and let it build your faith. Let it remind you that you, too, have a unique story full of significance that is going to make a necessary impact on this world.

MEET SARAH

Sarah is my younger sister. She currently lives in Montana with her husband who is a professional hunting guide. She works for the family business, preparing meals for the clients while her husband and father-in-law lead them on hunts throughout the bush of Alaska. She is a passionate, fearless, and God-loving woman who is continually growing in confidence of who the Lord has made her to be.

Being my sister, Sarah grew up in the same environment as I did. We lived in a Christian home with parents that provided us with a safe and loving atmosphere. Because of this, we were fairly sheltered, and with that came a sense of familiarity. Similar to myself, Sarah didn't venture outside her comfort zone much. She lived in fear most of her childhood – fear of rejection and disapproval.

As a child, she wasn't really sure of who she was. She lived in a fog most of the time – going through life unsure of who God created her to be. Her ADHD played a part in this as she struggled to think clearly, and distractions came easily. The parts of herself that she did know – her loud, joyful, and adventurous spirit – were kept fairly hidden.

She was afraid to embrace her true self for fear that others would reject her.

God entered Sarah's story at a young age, but her decision to fully give her life to him was a journey. The older she got, the more she realized that being a true follower of Christ meant being different. Although she wanted to follow him wholeheartedly, she also wanted to fit in. The two competing desires battled within her throughout her childhood. She vacillated between finding solace in God during the hard times to falling back into the trap of finding her worth in others. All the while, she was unaware that God was pursuing her and preparing for her to *truly* come home.

Eventually, she grew weary of the battle, so she decided to take control to see if she could find what she was looking for on her own instead of waiting for God. In high school, she latched onto a boy that had taken notice of her because he gave her the acceptance she craved. The longer she was with him, the further she strayed from God. At first it was exhilarating. She thought she had finally found what she always wanted, but then she saw her sin for what it truly was and began to feel trapped. She had been lured into a pit of sin and death and couldn't find her way out. Her world came crashing down when her sin manifested itself physically through a sexually transmitted disease. When all hope seemed lost, she cried out to God. To her surprise, he had been in the pit with her all along, waiting for this exact moment to rescue her.

Then came the biggest test of all. To grab onto God's hand to pull her out meant releasing her grip on the boy's hand, who had given her what she thought she wanted. She had given so much of herself to him and letting go felt like ripping her own heart out. But the Spirit filled her with faith and courage, and she obeyed in his strength. She ran with full reckless abandon to her Father's feet and gave her entire life to him. Although it was one of the most painful times in her life, it was also one of the most beautiful and joy-filled. God graciously gave her the acceptance she was desperate for and was looking for in all the wrong places. As soon as she surrendered her life to him, God started healing her heart and graciously began dealing with all the baggage she now carried. Throughout the process, she learned what it meant to fall in love with Jesus. She was the prodigal daughter, finally home and her Father kept giving her gracious gifts that she didn't even deserve.

Many months later, God healed her of the incurable. God had not only redeemed her life and made her new spiritually, but also literally by healing her of the STD! She wept with gratitude, feeling the full weight of God's love and grace fill and overflow in her heart.

Six months later, God brought a new man into her life. This one was different. He saw her for who God had called her to be even though she still had a long way to go. She had been freed from so much, but God was still refining her. This new man, Josh, had a vision for who God had created her to be all along. He loved her in a way that reflected God's love for her. Soon after starting to date, Josh proposed to Sarah and she said yes to a decision that changed the rest of her life. She stepped outside of her comfort zone and fearlessly followed Josh to Alaska and Montana to live a lifestyle completely different than her own. God continues to bless and refine her in this new and crazy life that she now lives with her husband.

Sarah was once full of fear and unsure of herself, but has now embraced who God has called her to be with courage and confidence. Because of this, she understands what it feels like to feel unimportant and unknown. She knows what it is like to be lost and not know who she is. This fuels her passion to really understand people's hearts. What makes them tick? What are their unique passions? What has God created them to do? She believes that to be known is to be loved, so she enjoys getting to know others on a deep level. She loves calling forth strengths and passions in people and encouraging them to take the leap of faith and to pursue what God has put on their hearts. She no longer walks around in a fog, but God has given her a clear view of the person that he has made her to be. She feels that he has slowly been awakening her heart to who she is, and she wants to help others experience the same awakening. In her own words: *"Understanding someone's passions are just a way to their heart."*

Sarah's "roar" is *awakening the hearts of others to be who God has created them to be all along.*

God continues to use Sarah's story in the family business. Whether that is sharing God's love with a client, showing grace and compassion to her new family or encouraging her husband in the desires God has placed in his heart, she continues to faithfully share her roar with the world – even if it is only from a small town in Montana.

MEET LAUREN

I met Lauren last year when my husband and I began attending a new church in the area. Her similar sweet disposition and our common love for all things artsy immediately formed a bond between us. Since then, she has grown to be a dear friend of mine – one whose prophetic words were a huge catalyst in the creation of this book. Lauren is a compassionate, joy-filled woman who walks confidently in the love and freedom of Christ.

Most of Lauren's childhood was characterized by two blended families due to her parent's divorce and remarrying. She went from being the youngest of the family to being somewhere in the middle. Although her parents' divorce wasn't ideal and came with its own challenges, Lauren loved having so many siblings. It made it really easy for them to entertain themselves, and because they got along fairly well, she always had someone to hang out with.

As a child, Lauren was silly and light-hearted. She loved to joke with her family, but was terrified of the spotlight anywhere else. As her older siblings started entering their teenage rebellion years, they began to tell her that one day she would be just like them. This was the first time she decided that no one would tell her who she would be. Watching her siblings' choices play out before her very eyes allowed her to avoid a lot of pain and heartbreak in life.

When she was 15, she was invited to church. Her heart was stirred and interested in the teachings she heard there. The following summer, Lauren attended a Christian camp where she made a new friend with a girl named Elisa. Elisa shared her testimony with Lauren and was bold enough to ask her if she had given her life to Jesus. Lauren hadn't. Later that week, they prayed together, and Lauren invited Jesus into her heart.

Waking up the next morning, Lauren knew she was different, and she began to live her life for God. This is when her journey of refinement began. The rest of high school was filled with learning the obedience of letting things or people go. She felt like she was made to be someone, but remained afraid to show that person to the world. Her heart cried out to love and care for others, but she was crippled by shyness or the fear that others would think she was judging them. There were other moments too, where she had to learn to let things go for the sake of who she was called to be, even if it broke her heart. Obedience was a tough battle, especially when it meant choosing God over people pulling her in a different direction.

After graduating from high school, Lauren entered college and her familiar environment was replaced with new people, beliefs, and ideas. She realized how weak her foundation was and she stopped believing in God for about a week. During this time, God felt absent and she couldn't hear his voice. After a long week of feeling alone, Lauren was invited to a new church. Upon visiting, she was overwhelmed by the presence of the Lord. It was here that she once again could hear his voice and feel his love. It was the first time that she heard the prophetic word that God had big plans for her life, and that he was going to remove her rough edges and breathe life into her again.

Shortly after her reunion with God, she went on a trip with YWAM to the coast of central California. It was there that she had to face the fear and crippling anxiety that would keep her from speaking up when she desperately had something to say. She was able to see that she was called to peace and a sound mind and that the only one that defined her was her Heavenly Father. She was able to let go of comparison and learn to love herself so that she could effectively love others.

Coming back from that trip, she knew that it was time to put her new mindsets into action. She joined a discipleship program out of obedience, but through it God built a deep foundation within her, and she was finally able to embrace the person God had created her to be from the beginning.

God continues to call Lauren out of her comfort zone and into her true identity – someone with bold confidence and victorious hope. He calls her to cease striving and to claim peace. He has given her a passion for the heartbroken, the anxious, the unwelcome, the outsiders and the creatives. He has given her a heart to see harmony among the Kingdom of God, producing a beautiful sound that echoes the love of Jesus.

Lauren knows what it is like to be terrified of speaking up when she desperately has something to say. She knows what it feels like to experience fear in the face of stepping into who God has called her to be. But through God's Spirit, Lauren has found freedom in Christ. Her tongue no longer is held down, but is free to speak up. To speak love. To be speak life. To speak identity. She now has confidence in the woman God has created her to be, and she knows that his victory is hers for the taking. In her own words, *"He is continually asking me to be bolder and to call on the power of the Spirit within me."*

Lauren's "roar" is *bringing others to a place of freedom in Christ through speaking life and identity into each person she meets.*

God continues to use Lauren's story to influence and impact those around her. Whether it is through the young adult's ministry she leads with her husband or through her job as a graphic designer, Lauren's truth-filled words are like a breath of fresh air to each person she interacts with. The way she walks in the freedom of Christ is a clear picture of the way the Lord wants all of us to embrace the love he has for each and every one of us.

MEET AMBER

Amber, along with her husband, owns the custom home building company that I currently work for. From the moment I met her at my interview, I could tell she had a heart of gold and the most welcoming spirit. Since working for them for over a year now, she has grown to be more than just a boss to me. She is a mentor and friend who is constantly reminding me of God's truth for my life and his unending faithfulness. Amber is a compassionate woman full of God's goodness and grace.

Amber grew up in a Christian home with loving parents and two brothers. Her older brother was born with special needs. Throughout her childhood, Amber learned from her brother to have great compassion for all people. Like Jesus, her brother doesn't focus on other's differences, but instead loves them for who they are. This had a huge impact on her as a child.

Despite the fact that there were many positives to growing up with a special needs brother, there were also downsides. Often her brother had to be hospitalized because of his various medical problems. Their parents had to put a lot of attention on tending to his needs and that was sometimes hard for Amber. Many family vacations and plans were interrupted for her brother's unexpected health issues. Fortunately, Amber was able to learn to be flexible and selfless in the midst of it all.

Similar to my own story, Amber accepted Jesus into her heart as a young child. Her family was very involved in the church. She always had a growing desire to learn more about God and was able to grow and develop as a believer through mission trips and her youth group as a young teen.

After marrying her husband, Brian, at the age of 20, they began serving together as youth leaders in their church. Their mutual passion for serving God and others motivated them to continue growing in their faith. When the recession hit in 2008, their residential construction business began to struggle. Going from having plenty of money to not knowing if they were going to be able to pay their bills or buy groceries forced them to rely on God for all their needs.

It was during this trying season that Brian and Amber learned to lean on God in a way they never had before. Throughout this time, they not only grew closer to God, but to each other. They began to pray together each day, asking God for direction in their lives. Were they supposed to shut down the business and look for other jobs? After receiving a prophetic word from one of their vendors telling them to keep going and that there was blessing coming, they decided to stick it out. It wasn't until two years later that their circumstances began to change, and they started to see the season of blessing come to fruition. Full of faith, they continued to fight to build their business back up with God's help. Over the last few years they have finally been able to live in that season of blessing that God had faithfully promised them years prior. While they still encounter challenges, they are now firmly rooted and know that they can trust God to bring a solution to every problem that comes their way. Throughout all this, God has taught Amber to be content in all circumstances and to trust him in whatever season she may be in.

Throughout this time, Amber was also walking alongside her mother who was diagnosed with kidney disease and passed away after battling for seven years. Being very close to her mom made this journey difficult, and Amber once again had to seek God in the midst of this hardship. This journey brought her a newfound appreciation for the gift of life. It also caused her to seek God and his word on the subject of healing. As Brian and Amber dug deeper, they discovered the power of prayer. They began to practice praying and laying hands on people. Since then, they have only grown in this gift and have seen many healed through the work of the Spirit and their faith-filled prayers to our Heavenly Father.

God continues to grow Amber's passion for others to be healed physically, spiritually, and emotionally as well as her immense compassion and love for people. From a young age, God began forging Amber's heart of gold. He has given her the ability to sense when someone needs to be loved and the wisdom on how to uniquely care for that person. It may not always be direct, but God uses Amber's story to give others a glimpse into his unconditional love for them as well as lead them into a deeper relationship with him. In her own words, *"My passion is to love people where they are at in life situations (good or bad) and in their faith journey. This love for people inspires me to also pray for them whenever the opportunity comes. I believe God wants us to have a life full of his presence in every area of our lives and I try to help those in my path to discover this truth."*

Amber's "roar" is *touching people's lives through the radical love and healing found in Jesus Christ.*

God continues to use Amber as a light to those around her, and her story continues to be a testament to God's faithfulness and goodness. Like a lighthouse, Amber's life emits a steadfast reflection of God's heart for all people. Whether it is through her interactions with clients and subcontractors at work or her willingness to pray with bold faith for healing over anyone who needs it, Amber's story is beautifully transforming and shaping the lives of those around her.

MEET BRITTNEE

I met Brittnee about a year ago after my husband and I started attending a new church. The first Sunday we went, she was singing and leading worship. Her passion for the Lord was so apparent, and I remember feeling so overcome by the presence of God. She introduced herself after the service and each word she spoke was filled with such life and sweetness. Later I joined a study she led about learning to seek God in the midst of health and fitness, where I got to know her heart and her love for the Lord on a deeper level. Because she has chosen to follow God's call on her life, she has impacted many – including myself. Brittnee is a humble, life-giving, talented woman of God who has thrown off fear and now walks in God's peace every day of her life.

As a child, Brittnee and her family moved every two years. Although her parents were super loving, they were also workaholics, which left her and her sister to themselves quite a bit of the time. During her middle school years, she struggled a lot with identity. She found herself eating her emotions in the afternoons when her parents weren't around. Sugar became her comfort and her singing talent was her way of making friends.

Throughout the span of a few years, Brittnee's family moved around, but was able to commute to the same church because they loved the community. It was here that a few of the older women took her under their wing and committed to praying for her. This impacted her in such a deep way and is a large part of the reason she is who she is today.

After moving away from this community, her family stopped consistently attending a church. It was in high school that she began struggling with an eating disorder. As a senior, she lost a lot of weight and became pretty popular as she received a lot of the lead roles in the school musicals. From the outside, she appeared to be thriving, but on the inside, she was dying emotionally, spiritually, and physically.

As a high school senior, Brittnee received a college scholarship for her vocals, but turned it down to be near Taylor, her boyfriend at the time. During college, she tried out for the worship team, but didn't make it two years in a row. In the midst of this disappointment, Taylor also broke up with her. With everything stripped away, God began to work on her heart. It was during this time that she realized that she had a purpose and that her identity was worth so much more than her talent. She took most of college off from singing and focused on organizing events and caring for people. In this time, God taught her humility and selflessness.

Soon after college, Brittnee and Taylor got back together and were engaged. Shortly after getting married, Brittnee was extremely discouraged with the extra weight she had gained from birth control and wasn't caring for her body well. This was when God began to really refine her and through this, he led her to a ministry that helped others find freedom in Christ. This was where she was first introduced to the Holy Spirit. After spending a day there, she was set free and healed of her eating disorder. From that day on began a journey of renouncing all the lies and generational curses using the new authority she now held in Jesus. In this time of healing, God promised her that he was going to make beauty from her ashes, and that she was going to lead others to the same freedom she had experienced.

Shortly after all this, Brittnee began leading worship at her church. Her gift of worship and her passion for health and fitness started to grow simultaneously. These two passions of hers began to mesh together as one passion to see others worship in authenticity in every part of their lives.

Brittnee's first pregnancy was a miraculous one. While pregnant, she had a spirit-filled woman from their church ask to come to their home to pray over her. Alarmed, but feeling peace, they invited this woman to pray. Later, they found out that she had miscarried. Despite the doctor's orders, they immediately began trying again for another baby. In God's favor, they quickly got pregnant for a second time, but two months before her due date, she went into labor. Miraculously, their son, Ezra, was born full term and in good health. What was even more of a miracle was that he was born on the exact due date that their first baby was scheduled to be born. This launched Brittnee and her husband into a new level of trust in God. From this, God called them to a new church. It was here that they were both baptized in the Holy Spirit, and God continues to use them both in miraculous and life-changing ways.

About two years ago, her second son, Brave, was born early and sent to the NICU for a few weeks. This was a traumatic experience for Brittnee, but once again God showed her how to have faith beyond measure and taught her the importance of speaking life over a situation. Brave is now a happy and healthy little boy that continues to remind Brittnee to consistently draw courage from her Heavenly Father.

God continues to call Brittnee out of fear and into his peace. She is no longer a woman of hesitation, but is filled with boldness. She is not afraid of the gospel. She is not afraid to share and be vulnerable about what God has done in her life. She now walks in confidence that the Lord is going to use her story to bring healing, freedom, and victory to others' lives through the work of Jesus Christ. In her own words, *"The cry of my heart is for people to know his freedom in every part of their lives and to grow in their faith so that they can see miracles happen."*

Brittnee's "roar" is *teaching others to worship the Lord in every aspect of their lives so that they no longer operate in fear but in faith.*

God continues to use Brittnee's story to transform the lives of those she interacts with. Her passion for each person to live healthy lives in true worship of our Creator is making waves in the world around her. When Brittnee enters the room, she brings authenticity and faith. Whether it is through leading worship on a Sunday or speaking truth into someone's life – Brittnee is a beautiful example of a woman walking in all that God has for her.

Wow. I sit in awe of these four women's stories and I'm reminded of my purpose in writing this book – to share the message that your story is worth telling. I hope that by reading these stories and hearing my own, you are encouraged and empowered to tell yours with confidence.

I pray that as you close the pages to this book, you will have a deep understanding of the truth that God declares your story unique, significant, and indispensable. I pray that you will learn to remove comparison from your life and walk in the freedom that you are a unique reflection of the incomparable God of the universe. I pray that God would reveal your significance and that you would be filled with his purpose for your life. And finally, I pray that you would know the depth to which he deems your story indispensable and that you would tell it with boldness, expecting God to use it in bigger ways than you could ever imagine.

About The Author

Heidi Sugden is a woman with gentle strength who sees value in the little things. She currently works as a full time interior designer, but her creativity extends far past her job as she enjoys painting, calligraphy, writing and more. She is passionate about helping others discover the value in who God has created them to be and empowering them to tell their stories with boldness and confidence. This is Heidi's first book.

E V E R Y **O N E**

global giving initiative

In pursuit of our mission to help people get their voices and ideas out into the world, we realize that others are concerned with more pressing needs. Finding creativity in every person is important work, but getting food, shelter, and dignity to individuals must come first. That's why Unprecedented Press donates a portion of book revenue to the Everyone Global Giving Initative whose goal is to meet the practical needs of individuals around the world and to share the love of Jesus. To learn more, visit *everyoneglobal.com*.

Thank You

The author and the publisher would like to express our deepest thanks to the following individuals who made this project possible:

2018 Patronage Program:

Jeff & Gayle Kraft
Josh & Sarah Chadd
Jed & Beth Soper
Nate & Kate Birdsall
Meiste Homes
Paul Vander Kuyl
David & Carolyn Fleis
Norma Watson

Indispensable Ambassador Team:

Karen Pearson
Steve Pearson
Sarah Chadd
Holly Knudson
Lauren Moura
Brittnee Blom
Andrea Mason
Aaron Mason
David Fleis
Beau Arlt
Becca Arlt
Nicola Kraft
Jonathan Kraft
Christy Mulder
Stacie Neview

Beth Soper
Kathy Walters
Mitch Sheahan
Mackenzie Sheahan
Kali Weeks
Robin VanConant
Monica Wittig
Kate Birdsall
Erin Bremer
Amber Meiste
Courtney Bellingar
Tori Saylor
Kaylie Klaasen
April Best

Writing Contributors:

Brittnee Blom
Lauren Moura
Amber Meiste
Sarah Chadd

Editor:

Thi Dalley

Proofreader:

Emily Carr Phelps

Other titles from

Unprecedented Press

40 Shocking Facts for 40 Weeks of Pregnancy
Volume 1- *Disturbing Details about Childbearing
& Birth* By Joshua Best

40 Shocking Facts for 40 Weeks of Pregnancy
Volume 2 (*Terrifying Truths about Babies &
Breastfeeding*) By Joshua Best

She Can Laugh - *A Guide to Living Spiritually,
Emotionally & Physically Healthy*
By Melissa Lea Hughes

Once Upon A Year - *Experience a year in
the life of Finn* By Joanna Lenau

Y - Christian Millennial Manifesto
*Addressing Our Strengths and Weaknesses to Advance
the Kingdom of God* By Joshua Best

Y, The Workbook - *A Companion*
By Joshua Best

Crumbs - *100 Everyday Stories about 100 People*
By Rose White

The River - *A 30-day Study on the Role of the Holy Spirit in the Church, the World and you* By Mike Nicholson

Unstuck - *How to Grieve Well and Find New Footing* By Danette Johnson

Still Small Moments - *What Parenting Can Teach Us About Growing with God in Every Season* By April Best

Merbles - *A classic rags to rocky crags, to blue bumdrops, to riches tale* By Matthew Kennedy

The Coffee Shop Gospel - *Where two or three are gathered...* By Dan Van Ommen

Landmarks - *A Comprehensive Look at the Foundations of Faith* By David Campbell

Half Everything - *The Curious Tale of a Creative Creature* By Joshua Best

All titles available from Amazon.com or from UnprecedentedPress.com